Creature Comforts

PEOPLE AND THEIR SECURITY OBJECTS

BY *Barbara Collopy O'Halloran*

PHOTOGRAPHS BY *Betty Udesen*

Houghton Mifflin Company   Boston 2002

For Teresa, Nathan, and Nana for their inspiration,
and for all who shared their stories

AND

For John and Patrick

—B.C.O.

Copyright © 2002 by Barbara Collopy O'Halloran and Betty Udesen

All rights reserved. For information about permission to reproduce selections from this book,

write to Permissions, Houghton Mifflin Company, 215 Park Avenue South, New York, New York 10003.

www.houghtonmifflinbooks.com

Book design by Lisa Diercks
The text of this book is set in Perpetua.

Library of Congress Cataloging-in-Publication Data is available for this title.
ISBN 0-618-11864-0

Printed in Singapore
TWP 10 9 8 7 6 5 4 3 2 1

When a child loves you for a long, long time, not just to play with, but REALLY loves you, then you become REAL.

— Margery Williams, *The Velveteen Rabbit*

Chickey

CHRIS, AGE 35

Chris was the lead singer and songwriter for the band The Presidents of the United States of America. He composes music for movies (*George of the Jungle*) and performs the theme song for *The Drew Carey Show*. He currently records and performs with two bands: Chris and Chad and The Giraffes.

When I look at Chickey, I see a thread back to my childhood. He's the only connection that goes so far back—a connection that's been incredibly constant. My childhood was great—idyllic, in fact. No worries, lots of yard space, and a younger brother. One Easter, my brother got Chucky and I got Chickey—two rabbits wearing hats and bow ties. I can't remember why I named a stuffed rabbit Chickey—it's one of those things kids do, I guess. But he's been Chickey from the start. Now that he's earless, he's definitely grown into his name.

It's funny how Chucky and Chickey have come to look like us. Chickey's thinner, more wiry—he's gotten way more use than Chucky. He's a world traveler and a hippie. He's even been to places I've never seen. I used to let my girlfriends take care of Chickey and they'd throw him in their bags while they traveled. At some point, my brother and I realized that Chucky and Chickey were naked, so we would make these sleeveless pantsuits out of tube socks. Now Chickey knows he's naked, but he doesn't care—he's definitely unashamed.

Chickey has his own band—The Giraffes. He formed The Giraffes with a few of my other stuffed animals: Munkey Sr., Munkey Jr., Barry the Bear, Yoko Glick—he's a duck on wheels. Chickey's little arms are perfect for drumming. I remember wishing so hard that Chickey would come alive and that I could talk with him. Now Chickey is a fixture in my recording studio, making sure I'm keeping in touch with my roots. He keeps me from getting too fancy. I just like him. I like his presence.

Chris

Bo

They are inseparable. Eliana's only eighteen months old and already she's worn a hole through one of Bo's ears with her rubbing.

Mom

Bakey

ANNE, AGE 37

I call him Bakey, but his real name is Bacon. He originally belonged to my older brother.

Bakey is truly imbued with the power to comfort me, like a dog you love; it's a source of security and love I can go to. I've talked about this in therapy.

My friends know all about Bakey. On occasion, I've lent him out to them for a couple of weeks, or sometimes I'll cut a little square out of Bakey and give it to them to keep.

Once, while I was touring in Arizona, I lent Bakey to a fellow actor who was feeling low. When I asked how Bakey was, he just shrieked "Oh my God!" Of course I knew immediately that he'd left Bakey in his unmade bed. I tried to hide how devastated I actually was. We had to go through all of the hotel's dirty laundry, but we finally found him.

I feel like Bakey's an entity, not a person but an entity that I can hug and hold and kiss whenever I feel depressed.

Anne

Anne is a graduate of Julliard who has appeared on Broadway in *Les Miserables* and *Miss Saigon*.

Banky

KATHERINE, AGE 13

If I had to share her like a meal, I'd say, "No way." She's just sort of a "nighttime snack." I don't remember when I got Banky; I just remember liking her so much. She would be lying in my crib and I would chew on her. I like the fuzzy threads to snuggle with, and the stringy ones are good for chewing.

I used to not tell anyone because I was afraid they would make fun of me, say stuff like: "Hey, did you hear that Katherine eats her blanket?" Now, I don't care what they think; she's my little blanket.

I think I took it a little too far, but Banky's my special thing. I can even do some cat's cradle with her.

Katherine

Blankie

JOHN PATRICK, AGE 9

Blankie's really fuzzy stuff—a bunch of string. I feel for just the right spot—I call it the Good Spot. You bunch it up on the Good Spot.

About every week when my little brother wets our bed, I ask Momma to wash Blankie.

John Patrick

For a while, I refused to mend Blankie. I wasn't going to sew it if he was just going to play tug-of-war with it the next day! But I relented. He begged me.

Mom

Ada

PAULA, AGE 36

Paula is a graduate of Harvard and a news journalist.

I got Ada when I was eight months old. His name is actually pronounced "Uh-Da." I remember, or think I remember, my siblings asking me what I was going to call him so I turned to my father, asking, "Uh, Da?" as in, "What do you think, Dad?" but my siblings misunderstood and that was it—that's how he got his name.

Ada was at my wedding and he's in some of my wedding pictures. He's been to Europe seven times and Asia a dozen times—I have pictures of him on the Great Wall. I take him everywhere—on assignments, on vacation, on humanitarian volunteer trips—except to countries where smuggling is a problem. I'm afraid they might take one look at his patches and cut him open.

I like to be with Ada when I fall asleep. He fits my face—he conforms to my cheek. He's there in that interval between when you are awake and when you are asleep, when thoughts flow, between the day and the dream. I think Ada likes that place.

Ada makes me feel peaceful and comfortable. I've always been pretty happy—even as a teenager. I think if you hooked me up to one of those monitors, my blood pressure and my heart rate would show ultra-calm when I'm with Ada. It's like he's Zen or Yoda, only he's really a stuffed piglet.

Ada has always been there, he always listens, he knows what I feel. He's not a toy; Ada's become a sentient being. By that I mean he's deserving of compassion and able to give compassion back. He is a soul with fur and patches.

Paula

Bubby

JAMES, AGE 8

Bubby's face is special. He has a big smile. The first time I saw Bubby, he was hanging on my crib and I kept on trying to pull him down, and when I finally got him down, I slept with him. You'll have to ask my mom what happened next.

He lost all his hair from being in the washing machine and under the covers. I've had him a long time, I've been cuddling him a long time, and I'll still have him a long time. He was my first stuffed animal.

James

This is still the most important relationship in his life.

Mom

Elsie

NELLIE, AGE 94

I love my doll, I wouldn't take nothun' for my doll.

It was 1971. Elsie was the first black doll I'd ever seen in Woolworths. It felt real good to get her. She's a beautiful girl. She reminds me of me when I was young. No, I wouldn't take nothun' for my doll.

Nellie

At last count, Nellie had ten grandchildren, twenty-seven great-grandchildren, and seventeen great-great-grandchildren. Nellie says, "They're still coming, though."

Becky

CLAIRE, AGE 3

She got a boo-boo! We fixed her up.

Claire

When British Becky crossed the Atlantic to become the constant companion of a sweet and rambunctious two-year-old Texas girl, this doll didn't know what she was in for. In her hand-knit outfit and with her fragile body, she should have been a "shelf doll," a look-but-rarely-touch decoration. Try telling that to a tactile, mischievous toddler whose style of play is full-contact.

It wasn't long before the endless wardrobe changes, tea parties, and occasional dunks into the wading pool compromised Becky's engineering. The fabric began to tear, most terrifyingly at her right arm, the limb by which she was most frequently transported. We tried traditional therapy, sending her off to a doll specialist who stitched her back together. It worked—for a while. Inevitably, Claire's love continued to take its toll, leaving no alternative: duct-tape therapy by Dad. Criss-crossing her torso a couple of times did the trick, but aesthetically it was a failure—imagine duct tape on a pretty doll like that, how could he!—until a solution was discovered in desperation: gauze, layer upon layer. Becky's body was a bit stiffer, but Claire had experienced boo-boos of her own and knew it was for Becky's own good.

Becky is again Claire's favorite partner in crime, and now they are more alike than ever: sweet and charming on the outside, tough as nails underneath.

Dad

Allen

MITCH, AGE 32

It was Allen's unique look of acceptance of the human condition that made me want to laugh, and to keep him. I was staying in a hotel in Atlantic City for a week. I had no car and knew nobody. When you're a comic on the road, you have one hour of full employment in a day and twenty-three hours of nothing to do but wander and pass the time. So I played "games of skill" in an arcade near the hotel. That's how I nabbed him. I won a lot of stuffed animals that week—the rest I sent to my nieces, but I just had to keep Allen. He had a look that was just too cool.

Now Allen travels inside my duffel bag. He waits for me in my hotel room. And after a show, if I feel lonely, Allen doles out some advice. He understands people's faults. He doesn't look down on them. He's wiser than most—but he's not as wise as he thinks he is. I like what he has to say, but I don't always want to hear it.

Mitch

Mitch is a stand-up comic who has appeared on *The Late Show with David Letterman* and *That '70s Show.*

Beary

KAYODE, AGE 12

It's kind of cool to have something you've had most of your life—being twelve years old and still having Beary. He's not like any other bear because, like, I pierced his ear and got him a Michael Jordan hat.

Beary doesn't seem like he's a stuffed animal. He seems real to me. My brothers remind me that he's not.

When I get really old, I'll give him to my grandson. But I'm not planning on getting rid of him any time soon. I'm kinda . . . sorta . . . attached to him.

Kayode

Jim Bob Jim Bob

TIM, AGE 8

His first name is Jim and his middle name is Bob and his last name is Jim Bob. My sister says it's confusing.

I would be sad if I lost him. I'll always have him. I'll always bring him around with me.

Tim

Binky

ZOE, AGE 7

For a while, I didn't know my mommy. Then she came. She didn't know what to do with me. She didn't know our language. She wrapped me in the blanket and walked me around. Wherever I went, it went.

Binky makes everyone feel good. I wish it was bigger so more of us could share it.

Zoe

Adoption is a leap of faith, a belief that somehow, through the mountains of paperwork and interminable waits, you'll get the right child— your child. And you secretly believe, you hope at least, that there will be some sliver of recognition: a look she gives you, a sound she utters. But that day in China when they placed Zoe in my arms, she just looked sick, very sick, and it frightened me.

During the next few weeks, I held her and rocked her and sang to her, and I wrapped her in this blanket that my mother had made. And that's when I realized that her being part of me and me being part of her had nothing to do with a look or a sound but rather a certainty, an absolute conviction that we, without a doubt, belonged together.

Mom

Black Sweater

AMELIA ROSE, AGE 9

My mommy's love is in Black Sweater. I think that because when my parents were splitting up, it was winter, and my mom wore it a lot. I'm sure I'll always have it. If I tore it or something, I would unravel it and make it into a blanket or something like that. I'd sew it into a quilt.

Amelia Rose

Black Sweater is a three-time hand-me-down originating from I don't know where: shrunken, misshapen, unraveling at the edges, soft, warm, and comforting. My baby adopted Black Sweater when our world was uncertain. It's true, I wore it often. She said it smelled of me. She said it was my love. She curled naked around Black Sweater as she slept and insisted on taking it to her dad's.

Today, Black Sweater is a treasure we share. I can feel Rosie's love, her humor, and her strength inside of it.

Mom

Doggie

SHANE, AGE 9

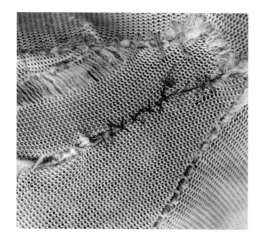

I got Doggie the day I was born. I was one month early. I was very small, but I was very tall. I remember when I was in my crib—I used to lie on top of him and I was just his size.

I bring Doggie to every hospital visit. When I'm not feeling good, I rub my face next to his. I use Doggie for a pillow. When they put me to sleep, I lie on him, and when I wake up, there he is.

I sew him up whenever I find holes. I ask my mom if I can get the sew box and she starts me out and I sew him up. I sew lots on him. He reminds me of my mom; that's the best thing about Doggie.

Shane

When Shane lost all his hair, he would say, "Doggie is on maintenance too . . . that's why Doggie has no hair" and "if Doggie can make it, I can make it." Doggie is definitely real. When you go through something like this, like chemotherapy, you don't have much that you are in control of. Doggie is Shane's comfort, the one thing that he does have control of.

When I look down and see this boy being comforted and cared for by Doggie, I know in my heart that Shane has the perfect love. I love to see his head lying on Doggie. How precious every single one of those stitches is.

Mom

Winky

JIM, AGE 50

I've had Winky about forever. I tried giving him to my kids, but they played with him so much it made me jealous. Now he stays under the nightstand on my side of the bed.

Jim

Jim is married, the father of two, and is a sales supervisor for a beer company.

Clarence

SANDY, AGE 30

"Clarence's Rubber Stamps"—that's what I wanted to call my new store, but no one would know who Clarence was, so I named it "Monkey Love" instead.

Everybody loves Clarence, even my boyfriends. Well, some say, "You're a grown woman, what are you doing playing with stuffed animals?" But if they're not nice to Clarence, they're out.

If Clarence could talk, he could write a novel. He knows all kinds of stuff about me that nobody else knows. I've cried on him I don't know how many times. He even gave me a Coach bag once. It was exactly what I wanted. I wonder how he knew?

He's a good monkey.

Sandy

Sandy is the owner of Monkey Love Rubber Stamps in Seattle, Washington.

Gorilla

DREW, AGE 41

I knew he was mine from the minute I saw him. I was a precocious reader—super into animals and especially partial to apes. I can still remember seeing him on Christmas morning. I just knew that no one else in my family could be getting an ape.

I really did love the thing. He was a constant companion, an active play friend. I dragged him everywhere. We made nests of leaves and climbed a lot of trees. I think that's how his paws fell apart. My mom was forever frustrated by having to sew Gorilla. Later on, when I was in medical school, I'd practice my stitches on him.

I love it now when children bring their stuffed animals to the clinic. I always examine the animal first. It really helps a lot when you're a two-year-old and fearful of the doctor.

I had forgotten this until my wife reminded me the other day: when I asked her to marry me, I gave her Gorilla. She wasn't quite sure what to do with him. I think I did that because I didn't have much else to give at the time and this was a very personal gift. This was a way of sharing my past. Besides, I knew she would give him back! I'm not very material—I'm not one to be encumbered by material things, but I always keep my personal connections.

Drew

Drew is a pediatrician who travels frequently to Africa, volunteering his time as a humanitarian healthcare worker and teacher.

Blanky and the Nippi Strips

JESSICA, AGE 18

When I was little, I would suck my thumb while rubbing my nose on Blanky's border. I did this so often that Blanky began to fall apart. This worried my mom—she thought I might strangle myself in the night—so she started cutting strips off of Blanky and giving them to me to use instead. We called these strips "Nippi."

One time I lost one of the Nippi strips. It flew right out of the car window. We must have spent a half-hour driving back and forth looking for it. We finally found Nippi hooked to the back bumper of the car!

I still have Blanky. My Mom keeps it for me in her "memento drawer" . . . but the Nippi Strips are long gone.

Jessica

Jessica is a college freshman.

Purple Blankie

KEIKO, AGE 3

Purple Blankie isn't really a blanket. From the time she was about six months old, Keiko could be appeased with labels on just about any article of clothing. Keiko would stick her finger inside the label and stroke her cheek with the silky fabric. Then one night, in a sleepy stupor when I couldn't find anything else with a label on it, I gave her the nightgown I was wearing. She hasn't let go of it since.

Once we misplaced Purple Blankie just before we were about to get on a six-hour flight for home. We finally found her in a side pouch, but of course by that time we had already unpacked the entire contents of all our suitcases right there at baggage check-in. Keiko yelled so loud that she unnerved her grand-father—which is pretty hard to do.

Mom

Blanky

LESA, AGE 19

Blanky is what I would cry into at night. I was so homesick when I first went to school, when I moved away from my hometown. I am very close to my family, and I guess Blanky reminds me of home and Mom and Dad.

When I was little, I had to take him everywhere. Mom would get so irritated. I remember my mom took me into a grocery store and Blanky was under all the groceries in the cart. I reached through the metal slats to touch Blanky and my hand got stuck. They had to make a call over the P.A. for someone to come rescue me.

Lesa

Lesa is a sophomore in college.

Doggie

ANDREW, AGE 11

Doggie is like a friend. He's always with me. He's just cool. I'd probably give him to my son, like a thing you pass down, but if he threw Doggie in a puddle or something, I'd take him back.

Andrew

Doll Henry

TOM, AGE 45

I don't remember how he got his name, but my middle name is Henry and my grandfather's name is Henry. He's just always been Henry. My sister got Doll Freddy and I got Doll Henry. Every year Doll Henry gets a card from Doll Freddy. We joke around that Doll Freddy is his cousin.

Doll Henry's body was made out of fabric, which was always ripping, and every time it ripped, we would put a Band-Aid on it. Well, eventually all that was left of his body were the Band-Aids, and finally even they disintegrated.

It never occurred to me to throw him away. Doll Henry has been a true friend all my life. I've owned some things I've had to question along the way—about whether I would throw them away or not—but not Doll Henry. He's my buddy . . . what can I say?

I've saved all his parts. I still have the stuffing. I've kept it all in a bag for thirty-seven years. I've always intended to replace his body, I just never got around to it. I intend to now.

When I smell him, I smell the house I grew up in. He takes me back to the '50s.

Tom

Tom is a first-grade teacher and a banjo player.

Carol

MACKENZIE, AGE 7

Carol

STEPHANIE, AGE 7

Having the same doll is nice; it's like we're sisters, we're so close.

Mackenzie

I am shy for people to see my Carol, except for Mackenzie. I love the smell of Carol. She makes me feel safe.

Stephanie

Suzie is like me: clumsy, small, and noisy. She does whatever she wants to, and when she gets mad, she gets really mad! My parents know that Suzie is special—they pretend with me. My dad makes Suzie report cards and gives her spelling tests. Once, after she got burned, my dad put aloe vera on her head.

Lily

Chocolate is nice. She's tall for her age. She cares about other people and is artistic. People don't know. They think they're just stuffed animals, but it's like they are real, like they're real people.

Lauren

My other friends keep asking, Are you crazy? I say yes—but I'm not the only one with a favorite animal. I'm not the only one who has something special.

Jamie

Suzie

LILY, AGE 10

Chocolate

LAUREN, AGE 9

Saundra

JAMIE, AGE 9

Blanky

EMMA, AGE 8

I used to have two Blankys. When we moved, I cut one into pieces and gave them to all my favorite people in the neighborhood. It was like a present that I was giving them. They could look at their piece and see the memories of me.

I love to sniff Blanky. I've spilled all my favorite goodies on her. When I get really sad, I come up to my bed and just lie down and smell Blanky. Then I feel better.

Emma

Nana

NATHAN, AGE 9

When I was little, everyone thought I was calling my blanket "Mama" but I was really saying "Nana." I love Nana and I love my mom. Nana's all ragged. I like her that way because I like to rub the stuffing inside of her; I like the little pieces that come off on my fingernails. If I lost her, I'd really be lost.

Nathan

I remember picking up Nathan from preschool and telling him what an exciting afternoon I had planned: a trip to the mall and then to the park. He let out this big sigh and said, "Mama, I just want to go home and be with Nana." He loves to sit and rub the stuffing inside his blanket. Poor Nathan—I don't know how many times his grandma would visit and, trying to be helpful, she'd sew Nana back up. I can still see Nathan's little hand trying to work its way right back inside.

Mom

Every day he took his blanket to kindergarten. He stuffed it into his backpack. I remember thinking, Why is he doing this!

Older Brother

Asi

MILES, AGE 12

I don't know how Miles got the name Asi out of "Blankie," but he did. It was quite innocent: a toddler trying to say his first words and the name just stuck, much to the amusement of all of us.

Miles was about three when his younger brother was born. As babies do, his brother would cry and scream, which was very unsettling to Miles. I would hear Miles trying to comfort the baby, saying "it's okay," but all that crying made him very nervous. Miles started chewing on Asi, actually biting holes through the fabric and tying it into knots.

This blanket went everywhere. I'd have to sneak into Miles's room at night when he was asleep, just to wash it. This mass of knots doesn't look like much, but Asi was such a part of my little boy's life; it's such a memento of his childhood.

I love how this ordinary object, this little piece of cloth, just stumbled into our lives and became such an incredible source of warmth, softness, and security.

Mom

Blanky

AMANDA, AGE 7

I like my Blanky cold. Once it was sunny and hot so I put him under the cushions of the chair. But I forgot. He was gone for about a month. I looked under the bed—he wasn't there. Then I heard him calling, "Amanda! I'm here, Amanda!"

Amanda